W9-AIJ-597

SUMMER
GREEN TO
AUTUMN GOLD

To Raul

Thank you to Dr. Dana A. Dudle, Winona H. Welch Professor of Biology at DePauw University, for reviewing the text and illustrations for accuracy

Copyright © 2019 by Mia Posada

All rights reserved. International copyright secured. No part of this book may be reproduced, stored in a retrieval system, or transmitted in any form or by any means—electronic, mechanical, photocopying, recording, or otherwise—without the prior written permission of Lerner Publishing Group, Inc., except for the inclusion of brief quotations in an acknowledged review.

Millbrook Press™
An imprint of Lerner Publishing Group, Inc.
241 First Avenue North
Minneapolis, MN 55401 USA

For reading levels and more information, look up this title at www.lernerbooks.com.

Designed by Emily Harris.
Main body text set in HandySans.
Typeface provided by MADType.
The illustrations in this book were created using cut paper collage with watercolor.

Library of Congress Cataloging-in-Publication Data

Names: Posada, Mia, author, illustrator.
Title: Summer green to autumn gold : uncovering leaves' hidden colors / by Mia Posada.
Description: Minneapolis : Millbrook Press, [2020] | Audience: Age 5–10. | Audience: K to Grade 3.
Identifiers: LCCN 2018047652 (print) | LCCN 2018048344 (ebook) | ISBN 9781541560994 (eb pdf) | ISBN 9781541528994 (lb : alk. paper)
Subjects: LCSH: Leaves—Color—Juvenile literature. | Fall foliage—Juvenile literature.
Classification: LCC QK649 (ebook) | LCC QK649 .P67 2020 (print) | DDC 581.4/8—dc23

LC record available at https://lccn.loc.gov/2018047652

Manufactured in the United States of America
1-44766-35703-1/22/2019

SUMMER GREEN TO AUTUMN GOLD

UNCOVERING LEAVES' HIDDEN COLORS

MIA POSADA

Millbrook Press/Minneapolis

red maple
honey locust
What kinds of leaves do you see in the summer?
linden
aspen
willow
ginko
bur oak
sugar maple

paper birch
silver maple
white oak
sweet gum
black walnut
dogwood
elm
cottonwood
ash

From **emerald** to **jade** and every shade in between, summer leaves fill the world with **green**!

The secret to their
green color is found
deep inside each leaf.

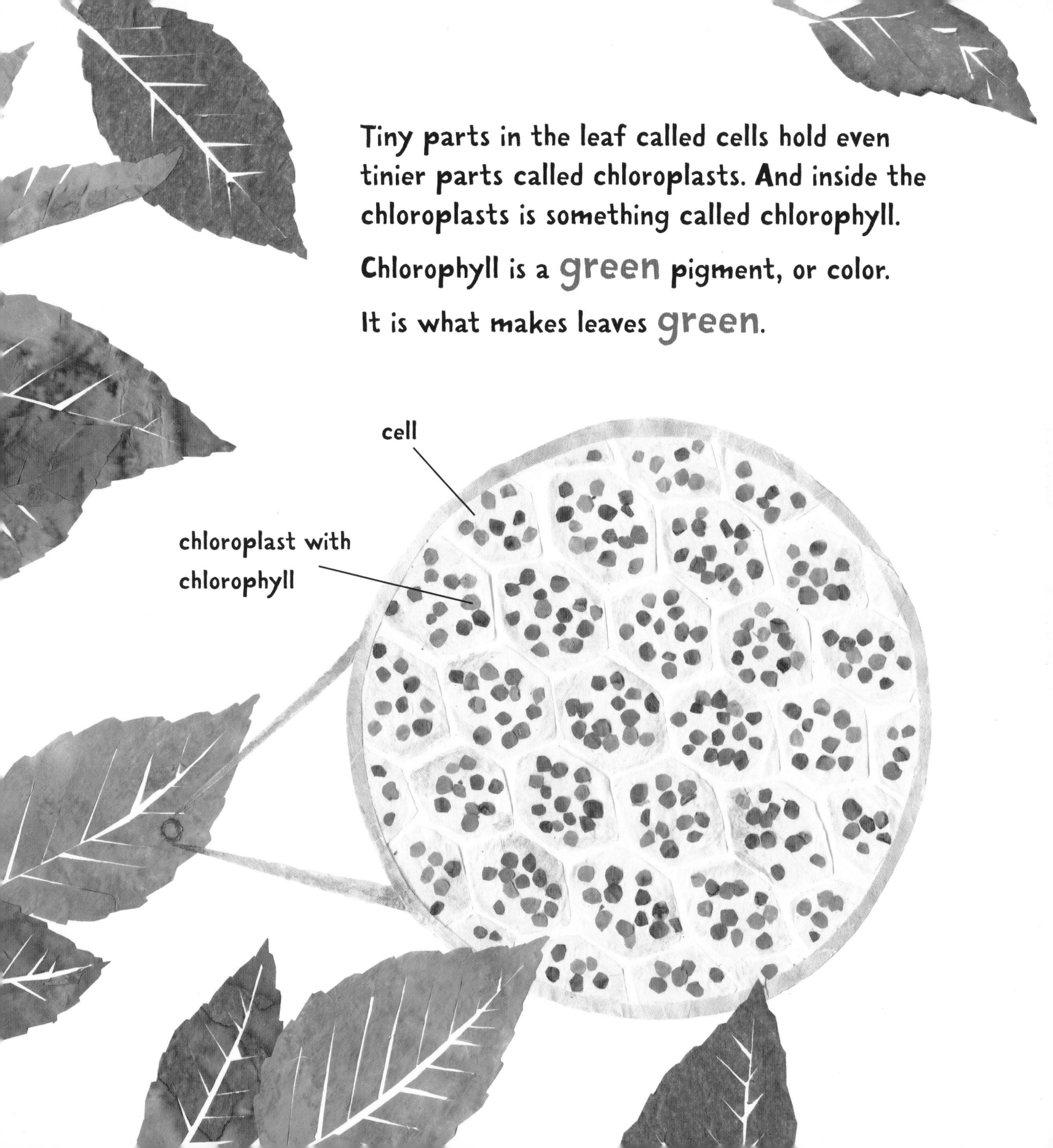

Tiny parts in the leaf called cells hold even tinier parts called chloroplasts. And inside the chloroplasts is something called chlorophyll.

Chlorophyll is a green pigment, or color.

It is what makes leaves green.

Besides making plants green, chlorophyll has a job to do. It helps make food for trees and other **green** plants.

When the sun **shines** on a plant's leaves, chlorophyll collects some of its energy. The energy combines with water from the ground and gas from the air to make food. The food helps the plant **grow**.

The green chlorophyll is also hiding something.

It is covering up other colors inside the leaf.

Orange and yellow pigments hide beneath the bright green.

All through the warm summer, they wait.

Slowly, summer ***creeps*** toward fall.

The air cools, and the nights grow longer.

These changes tell trees it is time to get ready for winter.

The growing season for trees is over. The leaves stop making food. They don't need chlorophyll anymore.

The chlorophyll slowly disappears, and the leaves' green color fades away.

Now the hidden yellows and oranges are finally revealed!

Some leaves turn **fiery red**, **deep purple**, or **bright pink**. These bright colors form inside the leaf as the weather cools.

Other leaves have brown pigments hidden inside. As the chlorophyll fades, these leaves turn **brown**.

Many leaves have mixtures of yellow, orange, red, and brown pigments.

The world is a rainbow of scarlet and orange, burgundy and gold.

Soon the stems of the leaves start to separate from the tree. The wind **blows** them loose.

They **drift** to the ground.

Piling up.

The fallen leaves **feed** the forest floor. They break down and become part of the soil.

They become food and shelter for insects, snails, and worms.

In spring, fresh leaves sprout from awakening buds, full of chlorophyll and filling the world with **green** again!

DIFFERENT KINDS OF LEAVES

The trees in this book whose leaves change color and fall off every year are called deciduous trees. Their leaves are soft and too fragile to survive a freezing winter. The stems of the leaves seal off to protect the tree from drying out and from infection. In doing so, the leaves are released.

Some trees, called evergreens, keep most of their leaves all year long. Evergreens such as pine and spruce trees have hardy needlelike leaves with a protective waxy coating that helps them survive the cold of winter.

PIGMENTS IN NATURE

The pigments that give leaves their vibrant orange and yellow fall colors are called carotenoids. Carotenoids are found all over the plant world. They are what make carrots and pumpkins orange, and bananas, corn, and daffodils bright yellow.

Red and purple leaf colors are made by anthocyanin pigments. Anthocyanins also make apples red and form the reds, pinks, purples, and blues of flower petals.

Brown colors in leaves are made by tannins. In early fall, the tannins interact with the carotenoid and anthocyanin pigments to create the golds, burgundies, and rich coppers in leaves such as oaks. Later in fall, the orange, yellow, and red pigments fade out of the leaves, leaving only the brown tannins.

Some or all of these pigments may be present in a single leaf. They combine and interact to form the vibrant spectrum of fall colors.